Bizarre Sig
& Odd Visions

Bizarre Sights
& Odd Visions

by
Simon Bond

Clarkson N. Potter, Inc./Publishers NEW YORK
DISTRIBUTED BY CROWN PUBLISHERS, INC.

Published by Clarkson N. Potter, Inc.,
One Park Avenue, New York, New York 10016 and simultaneously in Canada by General Publishing Company Limited

Manufactured in the United States of America

Library of Congress Cataloging in Publication Data

Bond, Simon.
  Bizarre sights & odd visions.

  1. American wit and humor, Pictorial. I. Title.
NC1429.B663A4   1983   741.5'973   83-4014
ISBN 0-517-54605-1

10 9 8 7 6 5 4 3 2 1
First Edition

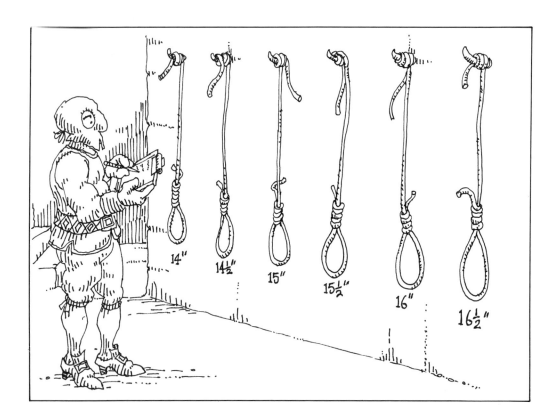

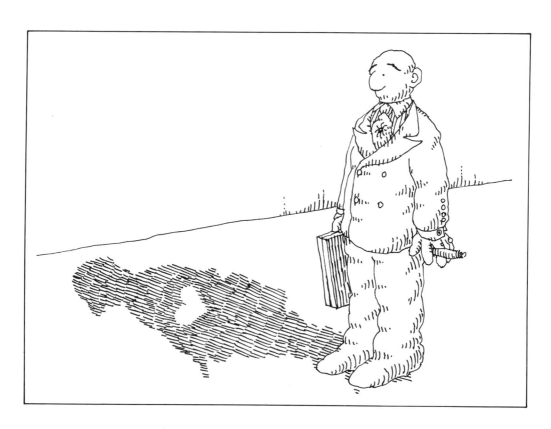

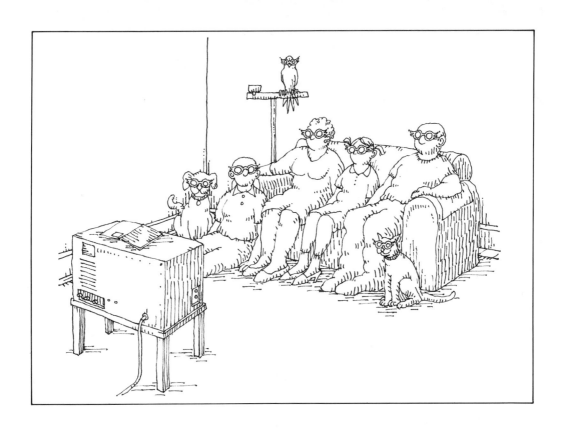

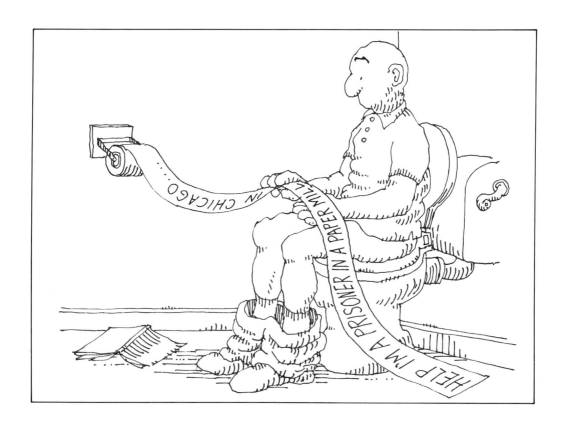

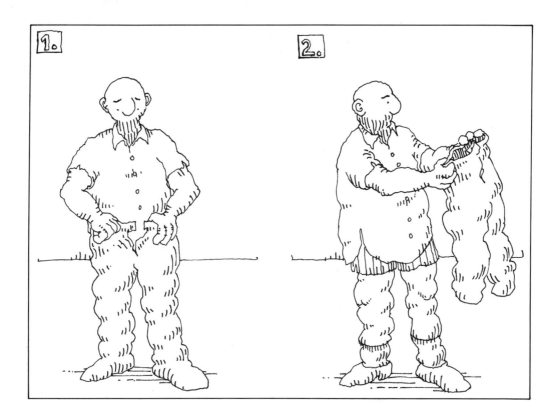

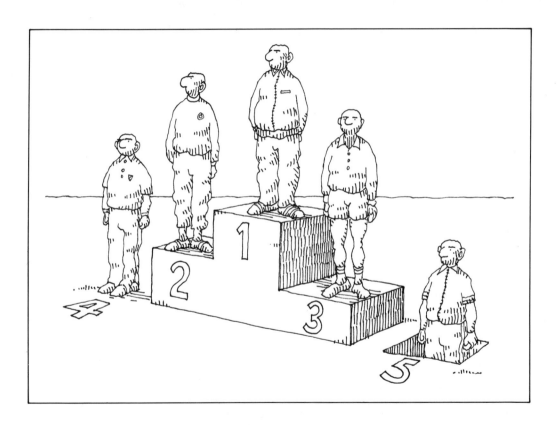

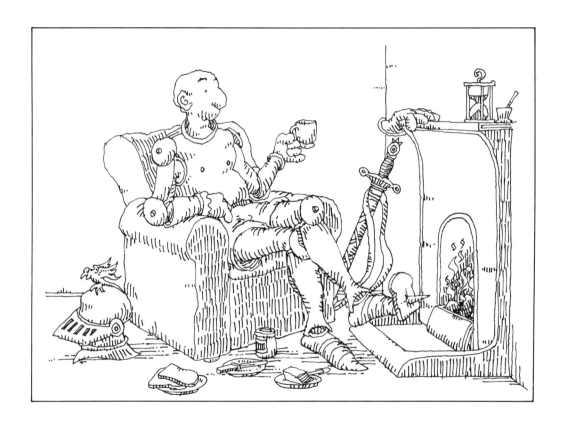

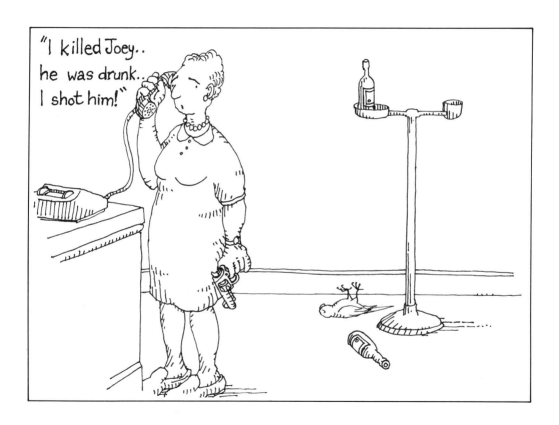

THE GREAT WALL OF CHINA
(THE GREEK INFLUENCE)

Abraham Lincoln
spoils the
Gettysburg
Address

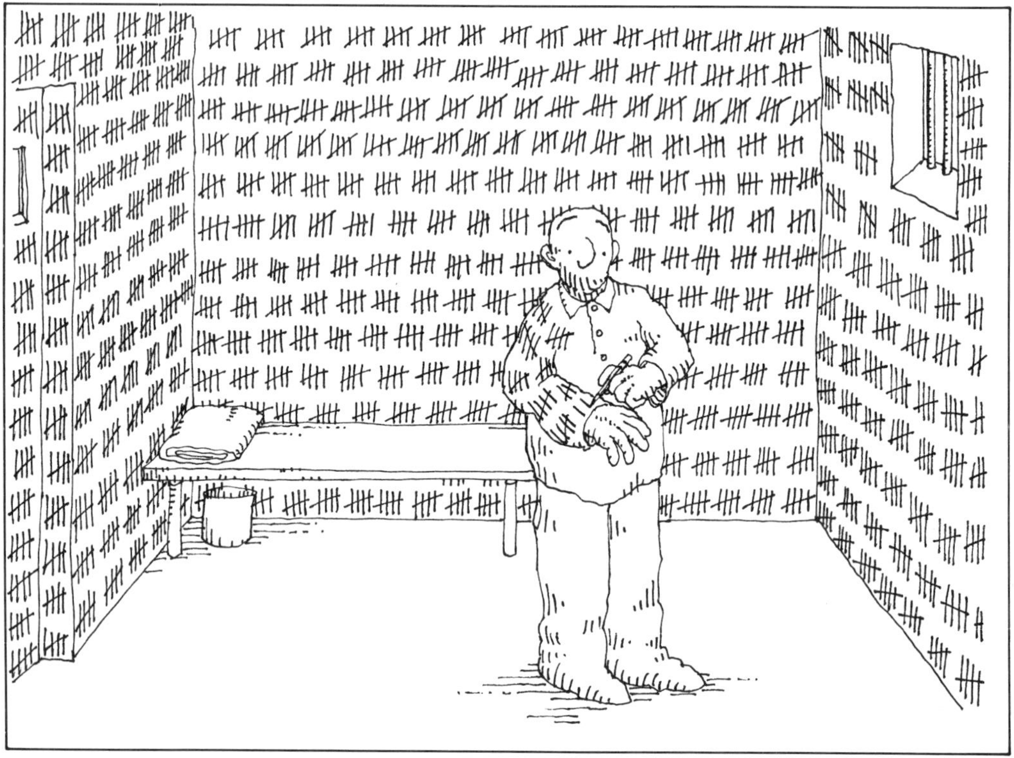

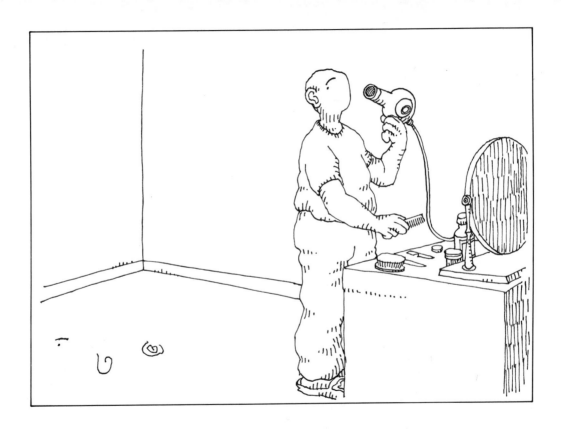

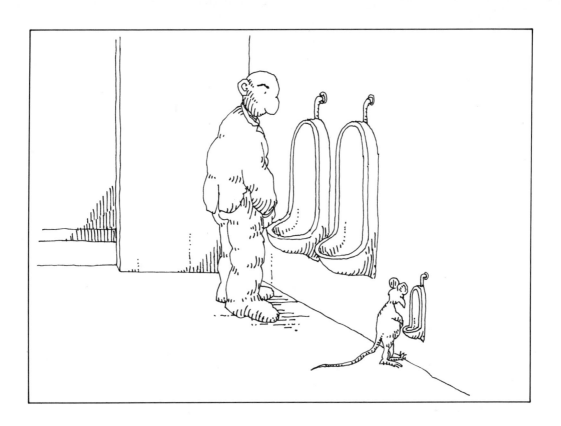

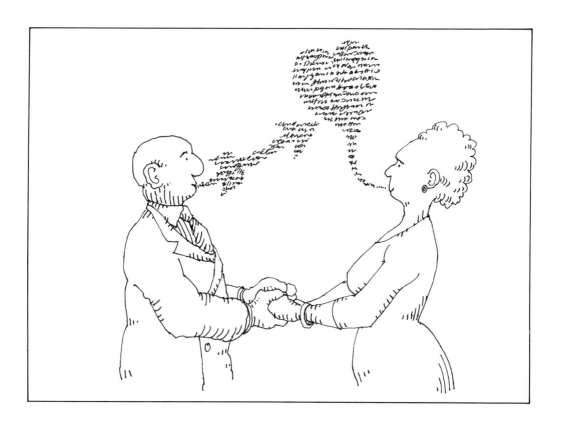

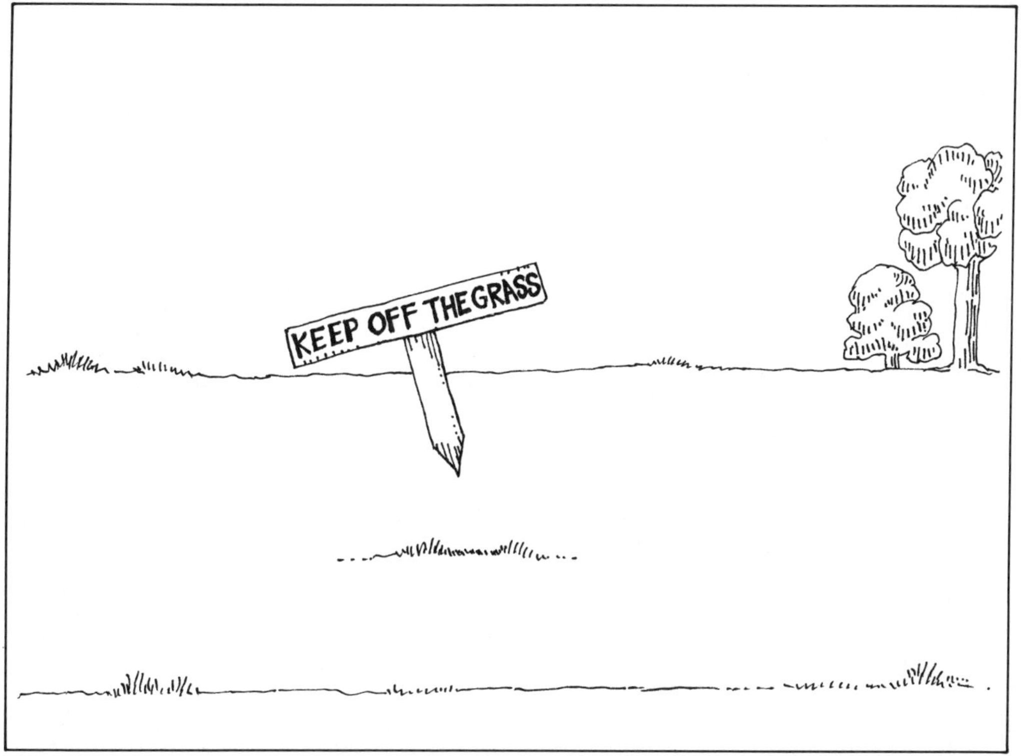
KEEP OFF THE GRASS

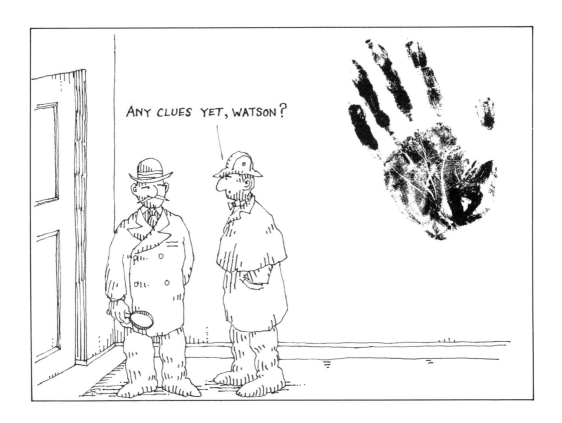

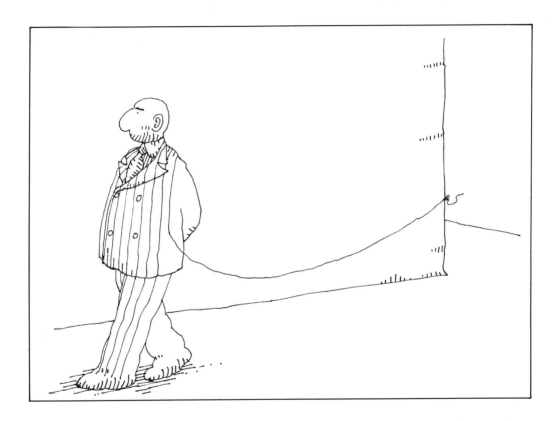

DEPRESSION IN THE DESERT

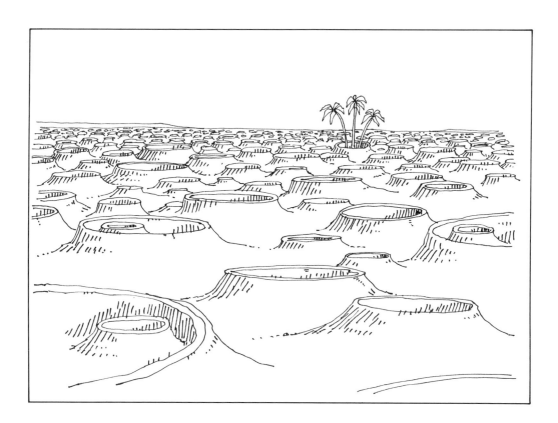

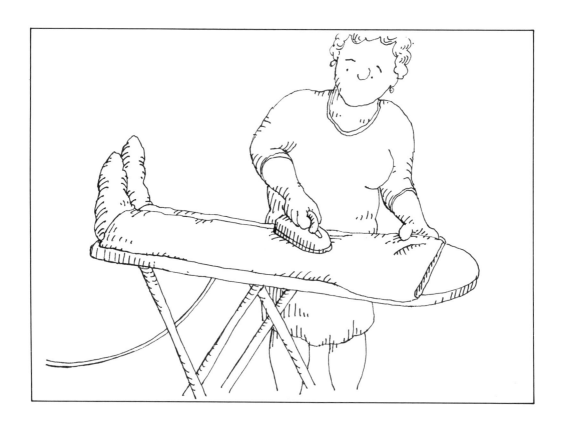

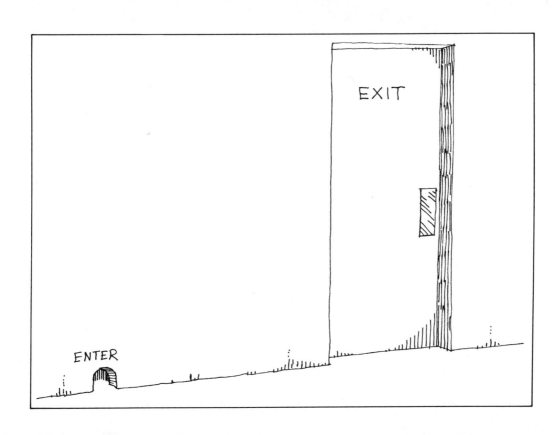

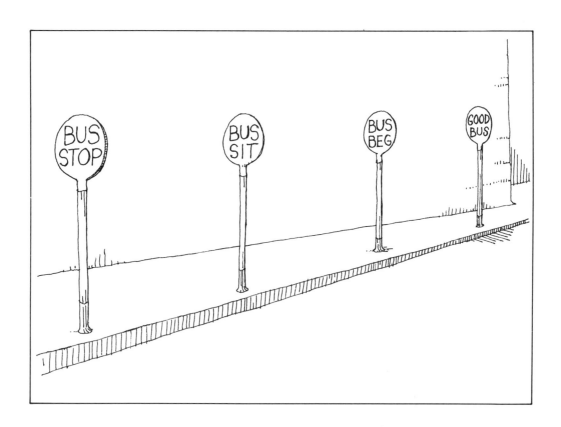

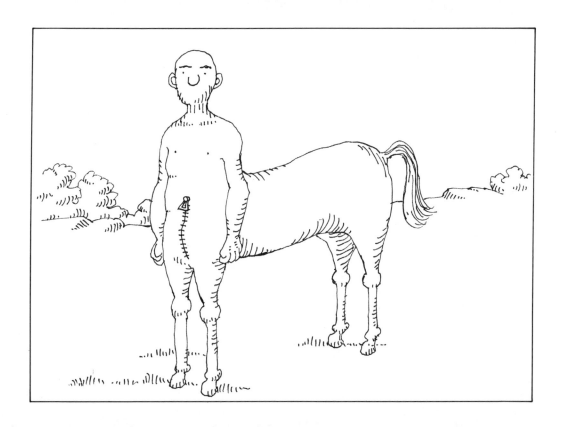

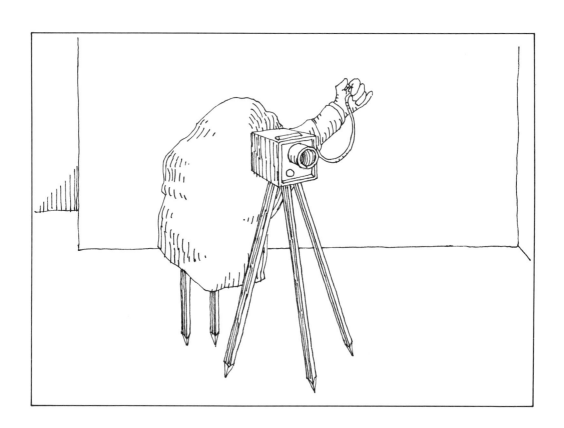

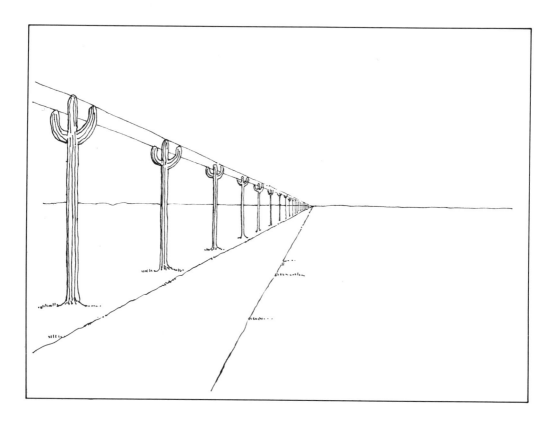

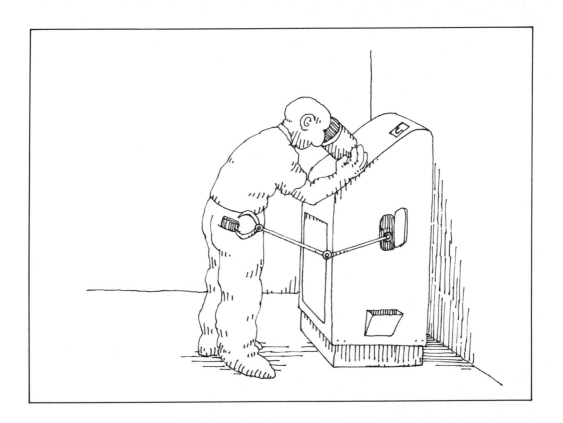

About the Author

Simon Bond is the creator of the runaway best-seller
101 Uses for a Dead Cat.

He now lives in a fashionable suburb of London,
where he is continuing his strange behavior but is at
least well dressed.